A Lick of the Spoon

Poems chosen by
Richard Brown and Kate Ruttle

Illustrated by Rowan Barnes-Murphy

CAMBRIDGE
UNIVERSITY PRESS

Cambridge Reading

General Editors
Richard Brown and Kate Ruttle

Consultant Editor
Jean Glasberg

Published by the Press Syndicate of the University of Cambridge
The Pitt Building, Trumpington Street, Cambridge CB2 1RP
40 West 20th Street, New York, NY 10011-4211, USA
10 Stamford Road, Oakleigh, Melbourne 3166, Australia

First published 1996

A Lick of the Spoon
This selection © Richard Brown and Kate Ruttle 1996
Illustrations © Rowan Barnes-Murphy 1996

Printed in Great Britain at the University Press, Cambridge

A catalogue record for this book is available from the British Library

ISBN 0 521 49993 3 paperback

Acknowledgements

We are grateful to the following for permission to reproduce poems:
'Hi, Coconut' by John Agard from *I Din Do Nuttin*. The Bodley Head, 1993. Reprinted
  by permission of Caroline Sheldon Literary Agency.
'Bubble Gum' by Tony Bradman from *Smile, Please!* Copyright © Tony Bradman, 1987.
  First published by Viking Kestrel Books.
'My Sweet' © Richard Brown, 1996.
'Drinking Fountain' from *Around and About* by Marchette Chute. Copyright © 1957 by
  E.P. Dutton. Copyright renewed 1984 by Marchette Chute. Reprinted by permission of
  Elizabeth Roach.
'A Lick of the Spoon' © Errol Lloyd, 1996.
'Scrumdiddly' © Robin Mellor, 1996.
'The Hardest Thing to Do in the World' by Michael Rosen from *You Tell Me*.
  Copyright © Michael Rosen, 1979. First published by Viking Kestrel Books.
'Yellow Butter' by Mary Ann Hoberman from *Yellow Butter Purple Jelly Red Jam Black
  Bread*. The Viking Press, 1981. Reprinted by permission of Gina Maccoby Literary
  Agency. Copyright © 1981 by Mary Ann Hoberman.
'Phew!' © Michael Smith, 1996.
'Into the Kitchen' taken from *Spot and I* by Patricia Maria Tan. First published August
  1982 by EPB Publishers. Copyright © Patricia Maria Tan.
'Harvest Festival' by Irene Yates from *Blue Poetry Paintbox*. Oxford University Press.

Every effort has been made to reach copyright holders; the publishers would like to
hear from anyone whose rights they have unknowingly infringed.

Contents

The Pancake

Mix a pancake,
Stir a pancake,
Pop it in the pan.

Fry the pancake,
Toss the pancake,
Catch it if you can.

Christina Rossetti

Betty Botter's Batter

Betty Botter bought some butter.
"But," she said, "The butter's bitter;
If I put it in my batter
It will make my batter bitter,
But a bit of better butter,
That would make my batter better."
So she bought a bit of butter
Better than her bitter butter,
And she put it in her batter
And the batter was not bitter.
So 'twas better Betty Botter
Bought a bit of better butter.

Anon

A Lick of the Spoon

I don't know
why my mum
bothers to bake,
for the batter
is better
by far
than the cake!

So give me
a taste
of the mix,
Mum.
Let me
feast
upon the spoon,
let me
scoop the bowl,
wipe it
clear
with my fingers,
then lick them
clean
to the bone,
one
by
one.

Errol Lloyd

Baby's Drinking Song

Sip a little
Sup a little
  From your little
Cup a little
  Sup a little
Sip a little
  Put it to your
Lip a little
  Tip a little
Tap a little
  Not into your
Lap or it'll
  Drip a little
Drop a little
  On the table
Top a little.

James Kirkup

The Hardest Thing to Do in the World

The hardest thing to do in the world
is stand in the hot sun
at the end of a long queue for ice creams
watching all the people who've just bought theirs
coming away from the queue
giving their ice creams their very first lick.

Michael Rosen

Phew!

on a hot day
on a really hot day
on a really really hot day
on a really really sweltering hot day . . .

there is nothing better in the whole world than
sucking on a
lovely
juicy
ice-cold
mouth-watering
tongue-numbing
melting
lolly
m
  m
    m
      m
        m
          m
            m
              m

Michael Smith

9

Chop, Chop

Chop, chop, choppity-chop,
Cut off the bottom,
And cut off the top.
What there is left we will
Put in the pot;
Chop, chop, choppity-chop.

Anon

10

Into the Kitchen

Into the kitchen
Sulin goes
With a chicken
And potatoes.

She puts some water
Into a pot
Then she waits
Until it's hot.

Into the pot
She puts the chicken,
While it cooks
The soup will thicken.

She adds the potatoes
And stirs the pot,
When everything's cooked
She'll eat it hot.

Patricia Maria Tan

Scrumdiddly

I don't like peanut butter,
but Dad won't listen to me.
He comes in and says,
"Peanut butter sandwiches, for tea."

And when I say,
"But Dad . . . ,"
he says,
"They're scrumdiddly,
they're spiffybosh,
they're extra scrumdidooshus."
And I know I'm out of luck.

I don't like dead green cabbage,
but Dad won't listen to me,
so every Wednesday we have
dead green cabbage for tea.

And when I say,
"But Dad . . . ,"
he says,
"It's scrumdiddly,
it's spiffybosh,
it's extra scrumdidooshus."
And I know I'm out of luck.

Dad doesn't like red ketchup,
so I put it all over his fish
and served it up like a waiter,
on a special silver dish.

And when he said,
"But son . . . ,"
I said,
"It's scrumdiddly,
it's spiffybosh,
it's extra scrumdidooshus."
And he knew he was out of luck.

Robin Mellor

Bubble Gum

I like to
Chomp, chomp
Slurp, chomp
Chew bubble
POP!
Gum but my mum says
Chomp, chomp
Slurp, chomp
It's a disgusting
POP!
Habit

I like to
Chomp, chomp
Slurp, chomp
Chew bubble
POP!
Gum but my mum says
Chomp, chomp
Slurp, chomp
One day I'll get in
POP!
Trouble

I like to
Chomp, chomp
Slurp, chomp
Chew bubble
POP!
Gum but my mum says
Chomp, chomp
Slurp, chomp
I look like
POP!
A rabbit

I like to
Chomp, chomp
Slurp, chomp
Chew bubble
POP!
Gum but my mum says
Chomp, chomp
Slurp, chomp
I'll blow too big
POP!
A bubble

I like to
Chomp, chomp
Slurp, chomp
Chew bubble
POP!
Gum but my mum says
Chomp, chomp
Slurp, chomp
I'll be swallowed up
POP!
Inside

I like to
Push, push
Poke, push
Chew bubble
– ?
Gum but can you hear me
Poke, poke
Push, poke
– ?

Outside?

Tony Bradman

My Sweet

Shall I tell you about the sweet
I'm going to invent?

When you first pop it in
you feel ten feet tall.
You look around the world
as if you own it.

And when you start to chew
your arms go Zing!
and your legs go Zong!
They're as strong as cranes.

And when you swallow my sweet
you can see over hills and seas
and into the tiniest insect's home.

You're a giant
with magic eyes.

Would you like one?

Richard Brown

Yellow Butter

Yellow butter purple jelly red jam black bread

Spread it thick
Say it quick

Yellow butter purple jelly red jam black bread

Spread it thicker
Say it quicker

Yellow butter purple jelly red jam black bread

Now repeat it
While you eat it

Yellow butter purple jelly red jam black bread

Don't talk
With your mouth full!

Mary Ann Hoberman

Drinking Fountain

When I climb up
  To get a drink,
It doesn't work
  The way you'd think.

I turn it up.
  The water goes
And hits me right
  Upon the nose.

I turn it down
  To make it small
And don't get any
  Drink at all.

Marchette Chute

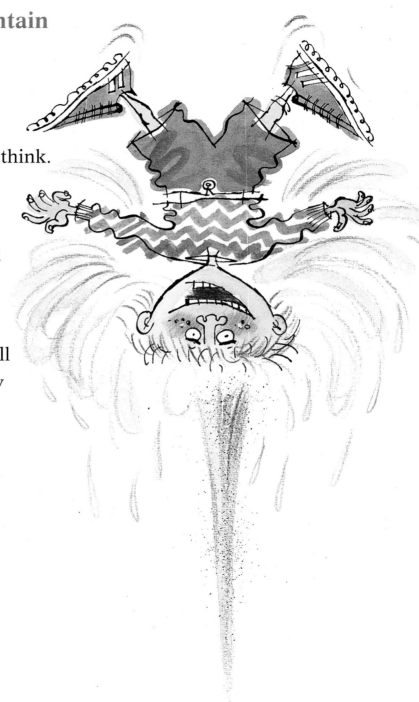

After All the Digging

and the planting

and the   pulling

of weeds

on hot summer afternoons

there are cool mornings

we can

walk between

the rows

and bite a bean   or chew a lettuce

leaf

and taste the ripe tomatoes

the

way

the rabbits

take

breakfast

Arnold Adoff

21

Hi, Coconut

Coconut tree
so tall and high
when I look up at yuh
I got to wink up me eye.

Coconut tree
yuh coconut big
like football in the sky.
Drop down one fo me nuh.

If only I could reach yuh
if only I could reach yuh
is sweet water and jelly
straight to me belly.

But right now coconut
yuh deh up so high
I can't reach yuh
I could only tell yuh

                              Hi,

                              Hi, Coconut

John Agard

Harvest Festival

Cabbages, cauliflowers,
crisp, crunchy swedes,
peppers and parsnips
and melons with seeds;
Onions and mushrooms,
potatoes for chips,
tomatoes, bananas
and apples with pips;
Stick beans and broad beans
and beans in a tin,
blackcurrants so juicy
they run down your chin;
Cornflakes for breakfast
and mangoes for tea –
Come to our harvest
and give thanks with me.

Irene Yates

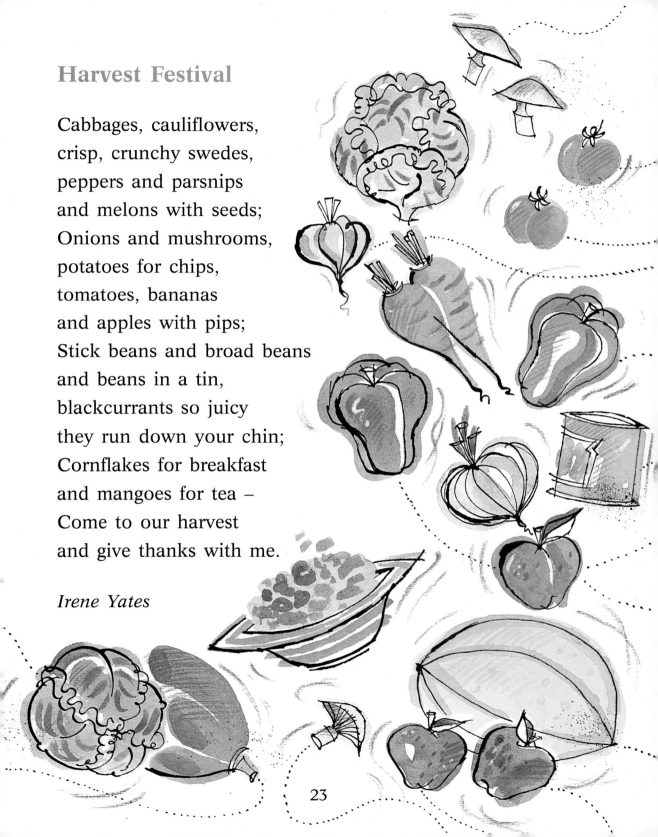

Index of first lines